BASIC BALTIMORESE II

An Illustrated Guide
For Getting Around
In **Balamer, Murlin**

Text by Gordon Beard
Cartoons by Mike Ricigliano

Copyright © 1990 by Gordon Beard
ISBN 0-9603436-1-X

To my wife, Joan,
Who understands Baltimorese,
but not my jokes

The dialect spoofed by this book is not universal in the city, but it is easily detectable as Baltimorese. While working in **Naplis** (see entry under N), I sometimes miss a more frequent contact with my hometown words. As a dynamic Baltimore prepares for the 21st century, Basic Baltimorese II is an affectionate reminder of our roots. **Balamer** . . . we love you.

William Donald Schaefer

William Donald Schaefer
Governor
State of Maryland

A Message From The **Arthur:**

Arthur? Sure, why not? I wrote the book, and in **Balamer** that makes me the **arthur.**

There . . . you've already had your first lesson in the peculiar dialect spoken in **Balamer, Murlin.** The words boldfaced in the text, and those depicted in the cartoons that follow, will provide additional examples of what you may hear as you traverse the city.

Obviously, not every citizen speaks the dialect. But once you hear it from the expert practitioners, best spoken in nasal tones, you'll not soon forget it.

Linquists and scholars have tried, without success, to pinpoint the derivation of Baltimorese. They have suggested various blends of Virginia Southern, Pennsylvania Dutch, Brooklynese, Allegheny Mountain English, Irish and British Cockney.

Whatever the origin, Baltimorese is a dynamic, living language with a distinct flavor. It flourishes in the 1990s, and is promoted as a sort of intangible tourist attraction.

Dan Rodricks, the award-winning columnist of the Baltimore Evening Sun, recalls that after coming to town from Massachusetts, a reporter called in a story about a body having been discovered in **Droodle Park.** That's the way it sounded, and that's the way Dan wrote it for publication; only to find out the caller really meant Druid Hill Park.

Mike Rhea, a native of Oklahoma and a former colleague at the Associated Press, was told by local authorities that a blaze was burning at a **tar** factory. The story was sent out before Mike discovered that the fire (**far**) was actually at a tire factory.

Another illustration, attributed to former Baltimore Mayor Thomas D'Alesandro Jr., may be apocryphal, but it shows what can happen when residents slur the name of Belair Road into **Blair** Road.

Legend has it that the late mayor, perhaps wary of a possible mispronunciation, once introduced Maryland's former Acting Governor Blair Lee III at a banquet as "Belair Lee." Reverse Baltimorese!

Is the story true? Thomas D'Alesandro III, also a former mayor, observed: "My father could have said it . . . go ahead and attribute it to him."

- ◯ -

The first edition of Basic Baltimorese sold 25,000 copies while serving as both a survival kit for visitors and as a refresher course and keepsake for residents.

The manual was distributed to members of the media covering the baseball World Series, the Preakness, and the presidential debate between Ronald Reagan and John Anderson (Jimmy Carter was a no-show).

Local firms have given the book as a memento for out-of-town guests attending banquets and seminars. Former residents send for them in a fit of nostalgia, or are sent copies to be reminded of their roots by those who have stayed behind. For tourists, the book is an invaluable aid to supplement their tales of Baltimore.

Basic Baltimorese II contains words not in the first edition, with two exceptions. **Oryuls** was retained because of the baseball team's hold on the area and its appeal to tourists. **Zinc** has been repeated, because I couldn't recall another viable "Z" word.

Reluctantly, I dropped my favorite Baltimorese word. It won't appear among the cartoons, but while you are in town, please think of me as you enjoy a piece of lemon **moran** pie.

Gordon Beard

A is for **ARTHUR**

A name once a king's,
We use to describe
A writer of things.

B is for **BAFFROOM**

Some go in a rush;
But one rule remains:
When leaving, please flush.

C is for **CRUPT**

One earns the label,
For taking a bribe
Under the table.

D is for **DUBYA**
A letter, you see,
The one before X
And just behind V.

E is for EHT
The past tense of eat;
When you're stuffed, it's hard
To stand on your feet.

F is for **FILLUM**
When you are in doubt,
Go to the darkroom
To see what comes out.

G is for **GUVNER**
But no need to bow,
You can pay homage
By doing things NOW.

H is for **HARBLE**

It can hardly get worse,
It's shocking, unpleasant
. . . And the end of this verse.

I is for **IGNERT**

A bit short of knowledge;
No one knows everything,
Not even in college.

J is for JOOLS

They're sparklers or gems;
No woman or girl
Should be without them.

K is for **KRODDY**

A Far Eastern art;
A kick to the jaw
Is one way to start.

L is for **LIEBERRY**

In "The City That Reads."
You should borrow the books
That can answer your needs.

M is for **MEZZALINE**

It's really no riddle;
Not upper, not lower,
But seats in the middle.

N is for **NAPLIS**

A town quaint and pretty,
The home of the Middies—
Our capital city.

O is for **ORYULS**

Fans go with the flow;
Don't try to pronounce,
Just give us an "OH."

P is for **PO-LEECE**

Our proud men in blue;
Just dial 9-1-1,
They'll come to help you.

Q is for **QUARR**

A group trained to sing
Cantatas and hymns,
Or, any old thing.

R is for **ROWERSKATES**

A Christmastime gift;
Go glide down the street
And get a big lift.

S is for **SORE**

But not one of pain;
No, simply a pipe
That some call a drain.

T is for **TUHMAR**

A day of surprises,
Only one thing is sure—
The sun also rises.

U is for **UHPAIR**
It's two words combined;
Some would say, "up there,"
So, hope you don't mind.

V is for **VOLLINCE**

Physical fury;
Explain to the judge
And to the jury.

W is for **WINDER**

A pane of clear glass;
To open or close,
Get off your . . . ah . . . duff.

X is for **X-LINT**

The top of the grade;
Come home with such marks,
You're made in the shade.

Y is for **YURP**

France, England and Spain,
A good place to spend
Your capital gain.

Z is for ZINC

In bathroom or kitchen;
When either overflows,
There's plenty of bitchin'.

There . . . you've survived a lesson in Baltimorese. As Casey Stengel would have said: "You done splendid." But to be on the safe side, tourists are urged to carry this book for ready reference.

Street and place names could still pose a problem. Following are some Baltimorese versions and their interpretations:

Blair Road . . . Belair
Droodle Park . . . Druid Hill
Dundock . . . Dundalk
Fort **MiKenry** . . . McHenry
Greenmont Avenue . . . Greenmount
Harrid Street . . . Howard
Igger Street . . . Eager
Lumberd Street . . . Lombard
Plaski Highway . . . Pulaski
Ricerstown Road . . . Reisterstown
Warshtin Monument . . . Washington
Westminister . . . Westminster
Wuff Street . . . Wolfe

Now, you're on your own. You should be ready for anything, so relax and enjoy the city. Remember, Baltimoreans are friendly and helpful . . . even those you have difficulty understanding.

List below any examples of Baltimorese you uncover:

_____

_____

_____

_____

Basic Baltimorese
5403 Plainfield Ave.
Baltimore, MD 21206
Phone: (301) 488-5403